# Jason and the Golden Fleece

*Written by C.J. Naden*
*Illustrated by Robert Baxter*

**Troll Associates**

# Pronunciation Guide

| | |
|---|---|
| Aphrodite | (af-roe-DY-tee) |
| Colchis | (KOL-kis) |
| Eros | (EAR-ahs) |
| Hera | (HEAR-uh) |
| Hermes | (HUR-meez) |
| Medea | (mih-DEE-uh) |
| Olympus | (oh-LIM-pus) |
| Pelias | (PAY-lee-us) |
| Phineus | (FIN-ee-us) |
| Poseidon | (poe-SY-dun) |
| Zeus | (ZOOSS) |

Great adventure stories are filled with danger and excitement, with fierce battles and impossible tasks. There are dreadful monsters and brave heroes too. The story of Jason and his search for the Golden Fleece has all of these things, and more. Some people say it is the greatest adventure story of all time.

The story begins when Jason was a little boy. His father was a King, but a weak ruler. He was so weak that one day the King's nephew, Pelias, took over the throne. Pelias was an evil man and he was powerful. Jason's father was afraid that the new King might harm his son. So Jason was sent far from the kingdom to grow up in safety.

The people of the kingdom did not like their new ruler. Pelias knew that, and he trusted no one. But a prophet told him not to worry about danger from his own people. Instead, the King was warned of a stranger who would wear only one sandal. This man would cause the King's death. Pelias was very frightened when he heard the warning.

One day, many years after Pelias took the throne, a stranger walked into the marketplace. Everyone stopped to stare at him. He was tall and handsome, well dressed and well spoken. But he wore only one sandal. His bare foot was brown and dusty. It looked as though he had lost the shoe a long time ago and had walked many miles.

When Pelias heard about the stranger, he was very frightened. He remembered the words of the prophet long ago. The King drove his chariot quickly to the marketplace. The stranger was there, talking quietly to the people. "Who are you?" demanded the King. "What do you want in my land?" The stranger looked at Pelias and smiled. But the smile was not friendly.

"I am Jason," the stranger said. "I am your cousin. And I have come to take back the throne that you stole from my father. If you do not return what is mine, I will take it from you." Jason's words struck great fear into the King's heart. For Pelias was a coward. He knew that he would not fight Jason. But he would not give up the throne either. What could he do? Then an idea came to him.

"You claim the throne, my dear cousin," said Pelias softly. "But surely a new King must first prove himself to his people. You have heard that many years ago the god Hermes sent down a magic ram. The ram's Golden Fleece is now held by the King of Colchis. But it rightfully belongs to Greece. If you can bring it back, you will also bring honor to us. Then I will gladly give up the throne."

9

Jason was thrilled with the idea of such a daring adventure. And Pelias was very happy because he knew that the young man would never return alive from such a journey. "I will find the Golden Fleece," Jason said to his cousin. "And I will come back to claim the throne that is mine." Pelias only smiled, for his heart was no longer afraid.

The first thing Jason did was to hire the master shipbuilder, Argus, to build the strongest ship that had ever sailed the sea. The ship was called the *Argo*. Those who sailed on it would be known as Argonauts. Great warriors came from all over the country to help Jason in his daring search for the Golden Fleece.

The ship was ready at last, and the adventure began. Jason poured wine on the ocean waves to ask the gods' blessing for a safe and successful journey. All the Argonauts knew that many dangers lay ahead. They knew that some would lose their lives. But they would find the Golden Fleece, and they would bring it back. Of that they were sure!

After many days of sailing, the Argonauts stopped to rest on an island. There they came upon an old man called Phineus. He was withered and frail, more dead than alive. They tried to give him food, but Phineus pushed them away. "I cannot eat," said the old man. "The mighty god Zeus has punished me for being too clever." The Argonauts knew that Zeus could be a jealous god.

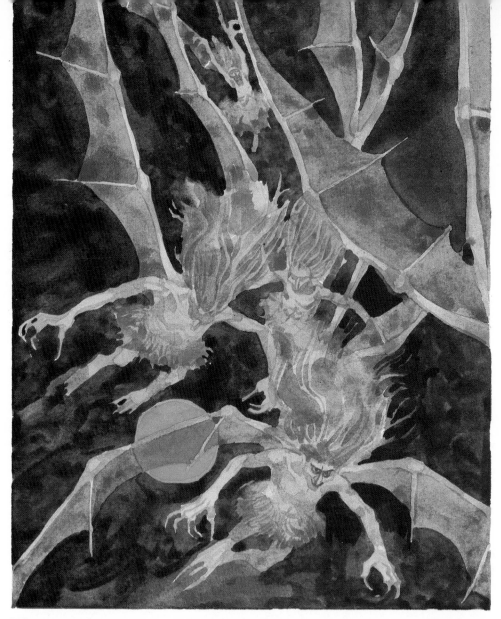

The punishment was terrible indeed. Every time that Phineus tried to eat, horrible winged creatures called Harpies swooped down upon him. They scratched and clawed until they ripped the food from his hands and flew away. Phineus could eat nothing at all. Now he was dying.

"We can free you from this curse!" cried two of the Argonauts. They told Phineus to put out food to eat, and then they waited. In moments, the dreadful Harpies swooped down from the sky and tore at the food. But the two Argonauts fought so fiercely that the Harpies flew away. And they never returned.

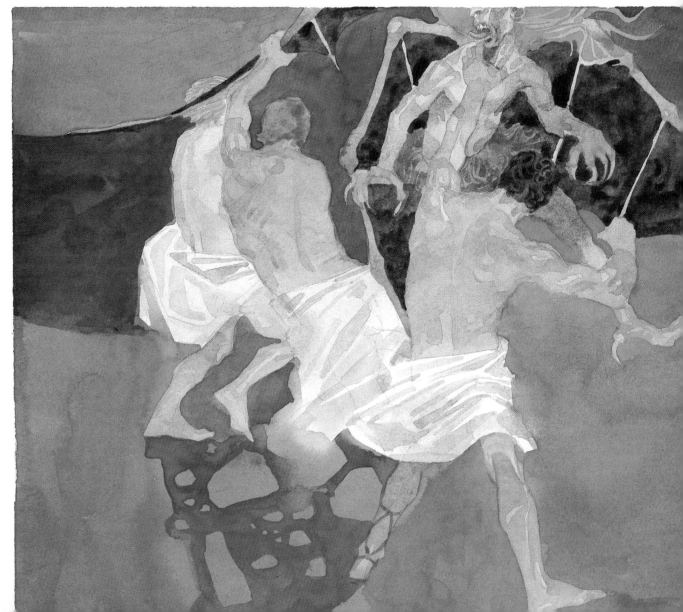

"You have saved my life!" Phineus cried. He was so grateful that he told the Argonauts the secret of the Clashing Rocks. They knew that to reach Colchis they had to sail between two huge rocks in the sea. These rocks smashed against each other without warning. If their ship was caught between them, it would be smashed to bits.

"Take a dove with you," said Phineus. "Release it when you reach the Clashing Rocks. If the dove flies through unharmed, follow it quickly. Your ship will pass safely, too. But if the dove dies, you must turn back. Your ship will be broken to bits if you try to pass between the rocks."

Jason thanked the old man, and the Argonauts sailed away with a dove aboard. Soon they reached the Clashing Rocks. They watched with wide eyes as the great stones smashed into each other with deafening noise. How could they sail their ship between them? Surely they would be crushed! Each Argonaut was silent with fear. Jason released the dove, as Phineus had told him to do.

The Argonauts watched as the dove flew slowly toward the rocks. It circled lazily for a moment, and then, quickly, it glided through unharmed. "Hurry!" Jason called to his men. "Row as you have never rowed before!" The mighty *Argo* cut sharply through the waves as the men pulled at the oars. Just as they reached the Clashing Rocks, the huge stones opened and the *Argo* sailed through. They were safe.

The journey to Colchis was long and dangerous. But at last the *Argo* sailed into the harbor. They had reached the land of the Golden Fleece. The King of Colchis came down to the shore to greet them. He was very curious about these strangers and their beautiful ship. "I am Jason," said their leader. "I have come for the Golden Fleece."

The King smiled at the young man's boldness. But he had no intention of giving up the Golden Fleece. So he said, "Surely you would agree that you must earn such a valuable gift." Jason nodded. "Very well," said the King. "This task is for you alone. You must harness my two fire-breathing bulls. Then you must use them to sow a field with the teeth of a dragon."

"When you have sown the field," the King continued, "the teeth will spring up as armed warriors. You must kill each one that attacks you. Then you will have the Golden Fleece." The King smiled again, but Jason's heart grew heavy. He knew that no one, not even a warrior as brave and strong as he, could do this impossible task. The Golden Fleece seemed lost.

But luck was with Jason. Sometimes the gods and goddesses, who lived on lofty Mount Olympus, came to the aid of mortals. And Hera, Queen of all the gods, decided to help Jason because she admired his courage. She called Aphrodite, the goddess of love. Together they told Aphrodite's son, young Eros, to shoot his magic arrows into the heart of Medea. She was the daughter of the King of Colchis.

Eros shot his arrows, and Medea immediately fell in love with Jason. Because she was in love, she decided to help him. Medea was beautiful, and she was skilled in magic. She gave Jason a powerful oil to protect him in battle. Then Medea wept because she knew that she was betraying her father. But she could not help herself. "I will not forget you," Jason promised.

The next morning Jason put the magic oil over his body. With Medea and the King and the Argonauts watching, he harnessed the fire-breathing bulls and began to sow the field. As each armed warrior sprang up, Jason struck him down with one thrust of his sword. Time and again, Jason was attacked. But he slew them all. Everyone but Medea was astonished. The King could not believe it. Jason had won the Golden Fleece.

But the King of Colchis was not ready to give up. When the Argonauts sailed away, with Medea and the Golden Fleece on board, the King sent his own ships after them. "Kill Jason!" he ordered. Once more Medea saved them. With her magic powers, she killed the King's warriors. But in so doing, she was forced to kill her own brother. Her sorrow was great.

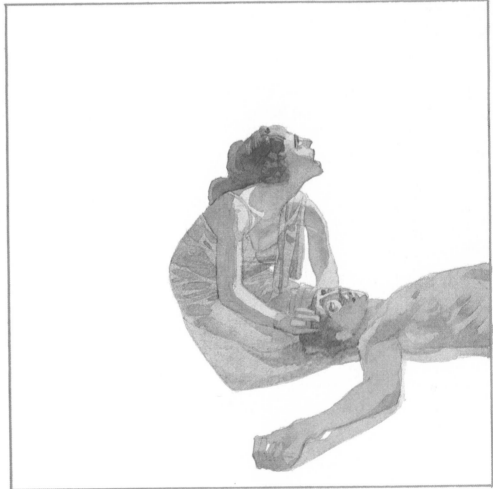

The *Argo* sailed proudly back to Greece. With the Golden Fleece in his hand, Jason claimed the throne from Pelias. But Pelias refused to give it up. He ordered all of his soldiers to protect him from Jason. But Medea had a plan. This time she used a cunning trick of magic.

First, Medea went to see the daughters of Pelias. "I have magic powers," she told them. "I can make your aging father young and strong again." Medea cut up an old ram and boiled it in water. Then she said some magic words. The ram sprang up, young and healthy once more. The daughters of Pelias were astounded. What a marvelous gift they could give to their father.

Believing in Medea's magic, the daughters of Pelias killed him. Then they boiled him in water. And they waited for Medea to say the magic words that would make Pelias young and healthy again. But, of course, Medea did not say the words. Pelias was dead. He would remain dead. And Jason was now the King.

Medea had saved Jason many times. But things did not go well between them. Sometime later, Jason decided to marry the Princess of Corinth. Medea was heartsick at this betrayal. And so she performed another trick of magic. Because of it, the Princess died. Some say that after this terrible deed, Medea fled to Athens.

Jason was a King, but he ruled alone. As he grew older, he spoke again and again of the daring and wonderful quest for the Golden Fleece. He dedicated the prow of the great ship *Argo* to Poseidon, god of the sea. Often Jason would sit beneath the prow, thinking back upon his marvelous adventures.

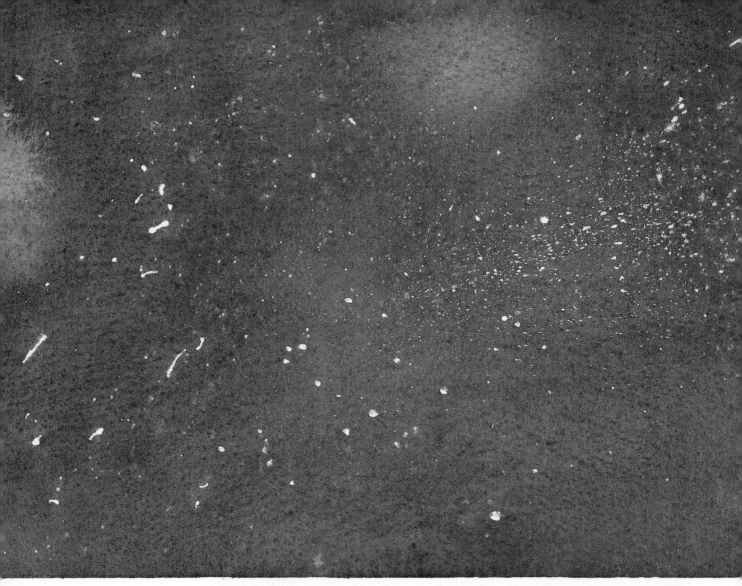

But perhaps the gods were unhappy with the way Jason had treated Medea. One evening, as Jason sat thinking beneath the prow of the *Argo*, it fell and killed him. Later, Zeus took the prow up into the heavens. He put it into the constellation of stars known as *Argo*. And there it would forever stay, a reminder of the glorious search for the Golden Fleece.